Praise for
BodyPrayer

"We are called not only to pray without ceasing but also to pray with our whole selves. *BodyPrayer* is a gentle guide to doing just that. Simultaneously subversive and traditional, the logic of *BodyPrayer* is holistic, anti-gnostic, and potentially transformative."

—LAUREN F. WINNER, author of *Girl Meets God* and *Mudhouse Sabbath*

"By sharing the rich prayer life of his Minneapolis church with the world, Doug Pagitt reflects a whole new way of looking at church—less in terms of 'what is your mission statement' or 'statement of faith' and more 'what are your practices and embodied rituals that are uniquely yours?' *BodyPrayer* is one of the first books to appreciate that embodied mediation is a key process by which theology is communicated and lived."

—LEONARD SWEET, author of *Out of the Question…Into the Mystery* and the trilogy *AquaChurch, SoulTsunami,* and *SoulSalsa*

"You can't get any more biblical than this! God created us to worship him with our bodies. Because of the Fall, God became incarnate to restore our worship of him. Because of a body that suffered on the cross and a body that rose from the grave, God redeems us to worship him—not in some disembodied soul but in, with, and through our bodies. *BodyPrayer* makes it real."

> —ROBERT WEBBER, Myers Professor of Ministry
> at Northern Seminary and author of *The
> Younger Evangelicals*

"This small guide to physical prayer is huge in its message. Doug Pagitt and Kathryn Prill return the body to its original place in, and importance to, Christian worship. We should all be grateful."

> —PHYLLIS TICKLE, compiler of *The Divine Hours*

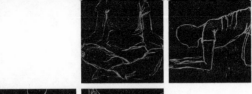

The Posture of Intimacy with God

BODY PRAYER

DOUG PAGITT AND KATHRYN PRILL
ILLUSTRATIONS BY COLLEEN SHEALER OLSON

WATERBROOK
PRESS

BODYPRAYER
PUBLISHED BY WATERBROOK PRESS
12265 Oracle Boulevard, Suite 200
Colorado Springs, Colorado 80921
A division of Random House Inc.

ISBN 1-4000-7148-8

Library of Congress Cataloging-in-Publication Data
Pagitt, Doug, 1966–
   BodyPrayer : the posture of intimacy with God / Doug Pagitt and Kathryn Prill ; illustrations by Colleen Shealer Olson. — 1st ed.
      p. cm.
   Includes bibliographical references.
   ISBN 1-4000-7148-8
   1. Prayer—Christianity. 2. Body, Human—Religious aspects—Christianity. I. Prill, Kathryn. II. Title.
   BV227,P34 2005
   248.4'6—dc22

2005015528

Printed in the United States of America
2005—First Edition

10 9 8 7 6 5 4 3 2 1

CONTENTS

Contents

ACKNOWLEDGMENTS

KATHRYN'S ACKNOWLEDGMENTS

Thank you, Doug, Colleen, Don Pape, and Ron Lee at WaterBrook Press for this opportunity.

Wonderful encouragement and inspiration have come specifically from Colleen, Jenny Jo, Eric, Tom, Melissa, Carla, Jenell, Rachel, Katie, readers of my blog, and my nephew Zachary. I am grateful to the community of Solomon's Porch for willingly and literally being contorted in prayer for over a year.

Gracias a Cory para los desayunos, para el café libre, y para las oraciones.

Sheraton, for all that's passed and all that will be.

In the simple and in the inexplicable, our Lord really is the Lord who reigns.

DOUG'S ACKNOWLEDGMENTS

I am ever grateful to the people who lead me, love me, and pray for me. First, my family: Shelley, Michon, Taylor,

Ruben, and Chico, you are the most important people in my life, and I am grateful for the time you allowed me to have my head in my computer as we worked on this book.

To the people of Solomon's Porch, who are the most creative and faithful people I have known, I love you all.

Thank you also to the wonderful people at Water-Brook Press for seeing the value of new ways to pray. Thank you, Ron, for your wisdom and input in helping my words make sense.

COLLEEN'S ACKNOWLEDGMENTS

Thank you...to my wonderful, supportive families: the Shealers, the Roberts, and the Olsons.

To my models, Maureen and Joy, for your patience and flexibility. To Stewart Luckman, for an ideal I will never obtain but will always seek. To my husband, Thomas Malcolm Olson, my gentle and true companion.

The Posture of Intimacy with God

Love the Lord your God with
all your passion and prayer and
muscle and intelligence.

The notion of the human body being involved in prayer is not a new one. It is, in fact, an ancient practice that is well documented throughout the Bible.

Christianity always has been a faith of the body. From its origins in the Eastern practices of the Hebrew faith to the life of Jesus to the great variety of expressions of Christian spirituality around the world today, it's impossible to deny the freeing truth that Christianity is to be lived in the body.

Central to Christian belief is the teaching that "God was pleased to have all his fullness dwell in [Jesus]."[1] Jesus lived as we do, sharing both the pain and the joy of being one of us. And before Jesus ascended to heaven, he promised his followers they would enjoy the presence of God dwelling with them and in them through the Holy Spirit. In us God continues to take up residence on earth.

Physical faith is an integrated faith, honoring both soul and body. Such an earthy spirituality was practiced by Jesus, whose life serves as the definitive model of physical spirituality. Again and again Jesus invested eternal meaning into ordinary acts, such as eating a meal with friends. When he performed acts of healing, he laid his hands on the person, and once he even used his own spittle to heal a blind man. In one of his most memorable ordinary acts, he knelt to wash the dirt off his disciples' feet. As I (Doug) wrote in *Reimagining Spiritual Formation,*

> These moments of physicality…give us permission
> to trust that God really is present in the mundane,
> physical acts of our own lives. God and the physical
> world interacting in harmony—this is the story of

Jesus. We see it in the birth of the savior through the body of a young virgin. We see it in the crucifixion of Jesus, which served as the coming together of the things of God and the things of the body for the reconciliation of all creation. We certainly see it in Jesus' physical resurrection, the great proof of the validity of his ministry. What Jesus did was not otherworldly, it was perfectly worldly.[2]

And Jesus invites us to live the same kind of life he did. As his followers, we are invited to "be his body on earth with our bodies."[3]

Christians have always lived a faith of the body, for the body, and in the body. Involving our body in worship, service, and prayer is more than empty ritual or mundane necessity. Engaging the body in acts of being present with God, including certain ceremonial practices, opens us up to God in new ways. People of faith in ancient times understood that such physical acts and practices as rest and worship, dietary restrictions, and mandated fabric in their wardrobes were of great value to their faith and life.

The practice of fasting, for example, is unmistakably

of the body. Similarly, walking a prayer labyrinth, going on pilgrimage, and making the sign of the cross have served to connect the physical body to the life of faith through the centuries. In any church today, physical practices such as taking Communion, singing songs of praise, and kneeling or bowing during prayer are common acts with rich spiritual meaning. Physical prayer and worship are so deeply embedded in the fabric of Christian faith that we can easily miss their significance.

- Many people are accustomed to closing their eyes and bowing their heads during prayer. For the originators of this practice, this was not an empty custom but a physical way of focusing on God. By their actions, these people of prayer showed that their immediate surroundings were not as important as God.

- For other early believers, folding their hands during prayer was a statement that they would not hold onto anything else when they were praying. It was a physical way to say to God, "Your kingdom come, your will be done in my life."

- Still others pray with their eyes open, their faces turned to the sky, and their hands spread wide.

This posture indicates a willingness to accept all that God has made.

- For pray-ers in the first century, it was common to pray facedown with one's knees pulled close to the chest and one's forehead touching the ground. Doing so put one close to the ground and in the most humble position possible.

- The custom of kneeling and bowing one's head in prayer is strengthened by the imagery of a person approaching a king to make a request. When doing this in prayer, the subject puts herself at the mercy of the King by exposing her neck, an act which shows her complete vulnerability to the Sovereign's power.

- The New Testament practice of placing hands on the one being prayed for is yet another physical act of faith and prayer.

- Still others pray while walking or singing or standing.

From the beginning Christians have recognized that prayer is not simply a matter of words; it is an integration of all of life, through the body. The use of the body in prayer is not just a long-held practice; it is a way of deepening our life of prayer. Just as nonverbal communication relies on gestures, tone of voice, and speed of speaking to reinforce our words, physical acts extend the meaning of our worded prayers. Physical movement and meaningful postures indicate more fully what is on the heart of the person who is offering prayers to God.

In addition to reinforcing what is prayed, physical prayer becomes prayer itself. Distance runners know well the experience of the body overcoming the mind's desire to quit in the middle of a marathon. Music lovers know what it is to be consumed by the feel and rhythm of a live symphony. Artists sense that their body is ready to create even before their mind is certain what to make. In the same way our physical expressions of faith lead the mind into deeper and more meaningful prayer.

In this process the mind comes under the reign of the body in a way that cannot be forced, and we experience a genuine connectedness between what we do and what we think. Physical prayer does not deny the mind nor denigrate the intellect. Instead, physical prayer puts into practice the recognition that we are whole people called and able to live complete, integrated lives with God.

We invite you with this book to discover ways you can enter into prayer that extends beyond the scope of words alone. Our hope is that the practice of bodyprayer will not only give you access to the rich history of people of faith but will also provide you means into a more integrated life—a life of faith, lived in the body.

PRACTICING THE PRAYER POSTURES

Bodyprayer is designed to help you connect with God at every level of your life—body, mind, and spirit. This connection is intended not only for your own benefit but also that you would be compelled to live the life of God in body, mind, and spirit for the benefit of others.

This book contains thirty bodyprayers. You may find that doing one per day for a month works well for you. Or you may want to repeat the same prayer each day for a week and use the prayers in this book over several months. You may choose to focus on certain prayers that speak to particular needs, questions, or desires in your life. (See Appendix B for topics.) Or you might prefer to pray according to certain prayer postures. (See Appendix C.) This book is meant to be a companion and a guide into deeper forms of prayer; this book is not a specific prescription of how prayer must be done.

Each of the thirty prayers has the following five components.

Introductory Thoughts

These thoughts give you some ideas to consider before, during, and after you pray. They are designed to set the prayer in context and perhaps provide you with direction as you pray. Of course, you are free to find your own meaning in the prayer.

Poetic Prayers

The poems are meant to be helpful but are not intended to substitute for your own prayer. Our hope is that the poems will supplement the prayer of your body without supplanting it.

The poetic prayers come in three kinds, each one identified by a symbolic icon: the face looking forward indicates a meditative prayer, the upraised face indicates a requesting prayer; and the face looking to the side indicates a prophetic prayer.

Meditative Prayers are statements of being. The word or phrase linked with a meditative prayer is intended to help you center your life on God.

Requesting Prayers are prayers of asking or pleading.

Prophetic Prayers propel us into the world to serve the needs of others.

The Prayer Posture

After the poetic prayer comes a description of a prayer posture. Feel free to practice each prayer in ways that fit you, but also consider being stretched in the prayer, literally as well as figuratively. Something in the suggested body posture may take your prayer to places you would not anticipate. But if you think of a variation of the position or need to change it due to physical limitations, please do so.

A Drawing of the Prayer Posture

A line drawing accompanies each prayer. The drawings are provided to give you a picture of what the posture can look like. They can also serve as a partner in the prayer: our hope is that when you look at the drawing, you will consider that others are with you in this prayer.

Prayer Journal

Each entry is followed by lined space for you to journal your thoughts or to write your own prayers. Use this space to make the book your own. Take the general prayers printed on these pages and add your personal pleadings, hopes, and dreams.

In addition, Appendix A lists passages of the Bible that you are invited to use in conjunction with each of the thirty prayers. These references were inspirational in the creation of the prayers in this book.

A SUGGESTED BEGINNING

We encourage you to consider starting each prayer in the same way—by separating yourself from the day's anxieties, worries, and pressures. Most of us maintain such a frenzied pace that we need a transitional stage to shift from schedules and deadlines to connection with God.

When we seek to pray, our tense bodies and racing minds often work against us no matter how great our desire is to connect with God. So before you begin to pray, you may want to reduce the tension in your body and to interrupt the frantic pace of your thinking. Deliberate and thoughtful breathing may help prepare you—both in body and in mind—to participate more fully in prayer.

As you begin to pray, close your eyes. Then inhale and exhale with deep breaths. Put your hands in a comfortable position—consider turning both hands palms up. Notice the tension in your head...and let it go as you take in a deep breath...and then exhale. Notice the tension in your shoulders and let it go, again by breathing in and then out. Notice the tension in your stomach and let it go. Move down your body doing the same. Once you have distanced yourself from the day's stresses, open your eyes and engage with God in prayer.

Ideas for Group Use

You may want to use these prayers in a group setting (as a church during a worship gathering, as part of a Bible study, or as part of a stretching class or exercise program). Here are a few hints for group use:

- As an opening exercise it may be helpful to read a section from this introduction or to share your own thoughts on why bodyprayer is important.

- Before you begin a posture, invite participants to take deep breaths and relax, separating themselves from the stresses of the day.
- Demonstrate the prayer posture and offer alternatives. Those with physical limitations may need either to remain sitting while others are standing or to place their hands on their knees instead of kneeling.
- Have the poetic prayer read a few times, perhaps by different voices coming from different areas of your meeting place.
- Encourage participants to connect with one element—with the poetic prayer, the posture itself, or even just the idea of engaging the body fully in prayer.
- Offer a time afterward for journaling, drawing, or reflecting on a verse from the Bible, a phrase that God has impressed on a person, or an insight that came during prayer. Encourage group members to let the idea from the prayer that sticks with them—whether it's the posture, the words that describe the thought behind the posture, or the poetry—expand in their mind. Have them let the

connection with the idea help lead them to pray
their own prayer.

- None of the poetic prayers ends with an official
amen, so participants may want to use bodyprayer
to lead to creation of art, their own individual
prayers, or a time of silence for reflection and
contemplation.

Please use this book with the freedom to mix prayers
with different postures or even to make up your own.
Again, this book is designed as a guide, not a prescriptive
set of instructions. May it help you pray and live with God
in body, mind, soul, and spirit.

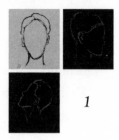

A Prayer of Kindness

Rubbing Hands Together Gently

God's kindness is often an undervalued reality of God's character. Too readily we think of God as powerful and awesome at the expense of remembering that God is also gentle and kind. The kindness of God is ever-flowing and ever-available, and it leads us to change. God's kindness is not a duty or obligation; it comes from God's very life. When we seek to live in the way of God, we must pursue love, joy, peace, patience, kindness, and goodness—for this is the way of God.[1] We pray and live as people who are kindly cared for by God; and we pray and live as the very kindness of God in the world.

The kindness that comes from the Lord
Identifies us as his own.
We must continue in it
Because we are God's children.

PRAYER POSTURE

While sitting, rub your hands together gently as if you were putting on lotion. Make sure to turn your wrists in all directions, and be sure to touch all parts of your hands—between your fingers, the backs of your hands, and even your wrists. Use a gentle, soothing touch, remembering that God knows exactly how you need to be covered in kindness.

PRAYER JOURNAL

_____

_____

_____

_____

_____

_____

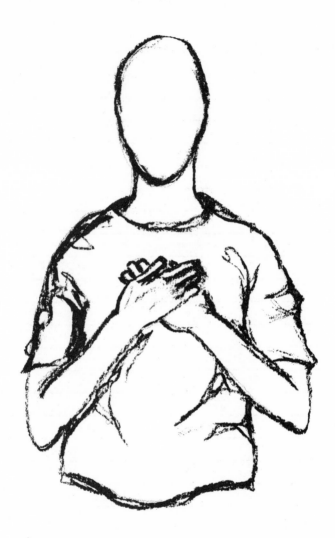

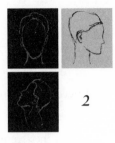

A PRAYER FOR STRENGTH

Hands Crossed at the Chest

The realization that we need more than what we have is a universal one. It comes in the form of thirst, hunger, cravings for relationships, and the need for faith. We need strength from outside ourselves as well as inner strength. We need strength in the times we feel weak and even in the times we feel sufficiently strong. We need to be people who pray for strength because we obviously need more than we have.

Fortunately we were born with an instinct to seek strength from God, who is willing and able to give it. So we pray for strength—not to become more independent but to recognize our interdependence on others and our need for God.

I need strength in my faith
To make the mountains move.
I need God's strength
To believe I am still seen by God.
I need the strength that comes from the Almighty
To walk in the paths he has left me.
I need your strength, Lord,
To be Jesus-like,
To be known as a follower of the Messiah,
To show the love you've given the world.
I pray and trust in this prayer and say, "Amen,"
In your name, with your strength.

Prayer Posture

Stand. Cross your arms high on your chest and let your hands encircle your upper arms. Cross your arms not as a posture of anger but as a reminder—by touching your arms—of the strength that already exists in your body. Stand with your feet shoulder-width apart and, if you like, bend your neck forward. Allow your crossed arms to be a posture not of defensiveness but a comforting reminder that the strength of God encircles you in all that you do.

Prayer Journal

_____
_____
_____
_____
_____
_____
_____
_____
_____
_____
_____
_____
_____
_____
_____
_____
_____
_____
_____
_____
_____

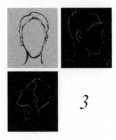

3

A PRAYER

OF ENJOYMENT

Hands Folded, Stretched Above Your Head

We are created to experience pleasure and enjoyment. These are not distractions from a life lived well with God; they are a gift from God. To enjoy God and life is a goal that is well-suited for humanity. This enjoyment must never come by giving rise to another's suffering, and enjoyment is never meant to be the sole purpose of life. But God designed us to enjoy, to relish, to laugh. So we pray and live, seeking life to its fullest, for all humankind and for ourselves.[1] As we enjoy life and participate with others who enjoy life, we honor the Creator of life.

> May the Lord be praised
> From now and evermore.
> We are blessed by his redemption
> And filled with his love.
> May the Lord be praised
> From now and evermore.

PRAYER POSTURE

Standing, clasp your hands by interlocking your fingers, then stretch your arms over your head. As you stretch upward, reaching above you, contemplate the joy and pleasure that God has built into life for your delight.

PRAYER JOURNAL

_____

_____

_____

_____

_____

_____

_____

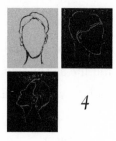

4

A Prayer of Re-Creation

Arms Open

God is never finished with creation, and God is never finished with us. We are constantly being re-created, and we are invited to join God as co-re-creators of the world. This re-creation happens in our attitudes and spirits as much as in the physical world. We re-create when we replace hate with love, hurt with healing, despair with hope. Our prayers beckon re-creation. We join this re-creation as we ask God to do anew in us what God has done throughout time. We pray for sight returned, babies born, lives revived. We seek mercy unmasked, love unimpeded, and faith remade. We join with all creation in seeking re-creation. For we know that all creation groans in anticipation of being remade. And we join in the groaning, to be released from pain and suffering.[1] We wait for God to give us our full life as children, including renewed bodies; we eagerly look forward to this freedom.[2]

> I wait.
> I wait for peace.
> I wait for what Jesus promised.
> I wait in my schedules, in my agendas,
> > in my life's routine.
> I wait and I extend my hope
> To believe
> That God will deliver me
> And I will be made new.

Prayer Posture

Standing, lift your arms out and up in a V position. Drop your shoulders, stiffen your fingers, and stretch by pushing up through your elbows and forearms. Reach toward God, the One who remakes and re-creates all of creation. Reflect on God's ongoing work of re-creation in your life and in the lives of those around you.

PRAYER JOURNAL

_____

_____

_____

_____

_____

_____

_____

_____

_____

_____

_____

_____

_____

_____

_____

_____

_____

_____

_____

_____

_____

_____

_____

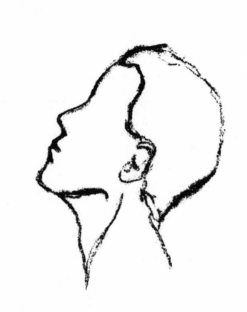

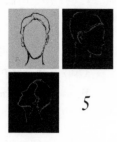

5

A PRAYER

OF HOPEFULNESS

Looking Up

Faith, hope, and love come from the same Origin—
God.[1] There are few things we need more than hope.
Hope allows us to trust beyond what we see with our eyes
and to connect with that which we know in our very being
must be true. Hope doesn't fail; rather it lifts up. Hope is
not wishful thinking; it is a deep knowing. Hope is not a
vain attempt to make things seem better than they are; it
is knowing that things are more than they seem. Hope
springs life, and life eternal. Praying and living as hopeful
people, may we be mindful of those who need hope and
do not have it. May we have hope for those who lack hope.

God of God, Light of Light.
Holy is our Lord of Life.
Bless me with hope as one of your own.

Prayer Posture

Stand or sit. Look up to the ceiling or the sky. Let the rest of your body relax while you feel the strain in your eyes. Contemplate the hope that comes from God: the hope that is unseen, yet eternally real.

Prayer Journal

_____
_____
_____
_____
_____
_____
_____
_____
_____
_____
_____
_____
_____
_____
_____
_____
_____
_____
_____
_____
_____
_____
_____
_____
_____
_____
_____

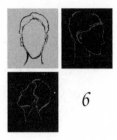

6

A PRAYER OF PRAISE

Pressing Fingertips

To praise is to recognize something as being of great worth. When we praise something, we say that it deserves notice and acclaim. To praise God is to join in agreement with all of creation on the goodness and grandeur of God. Praise is not self-generated flattery but our rightful response to God in light of the wonder of God. When we praise God, we are expressing relationship. That is, we do not praise God as lowly outsiders, but as those created in the image of God and recognizing in our being the majesty of God.[1] We praise God because we are certain of the majesty and wonder of God, a majesty and wonder that we know firsthand.[2]

Hallelujah!
Give praise to the Lord our God
For God gives mercy to his people.

Prayer Posture

While sitting, position your hands with your fingers spread and each palm facing the other. Gently press all of your fingertips together so you can feel your pulse in your fingertips. Slowly lift each fingertip off its mate, one by one. Work through your whole hand (pinky to thumb or in reverse). Then press each pair of fingertips together again, one by one. There is a theory that pressing each fingertip to its corresponding fingertip activates a certain portion of our brain. Also, it is one of the gentlest ways to feel our own pulse. Lastly, with our fingers, most of us as children "built" our first church ("Here is the church, here is the steeple, open the doors, see all the people!"). Allow yourself to indulge in the inspiration of your choice—activating your brain, feeling your pulse, or revisiting the time you "made" your first church—while you praise God with the largest area of nerves in your body.

Prayer Journal

_____
_____
_____
_____
_____
_____
_____
_____
_____
_____
_____
_____
_____
_____
_____
_____
_____
_____
_____
_____
_____
_____

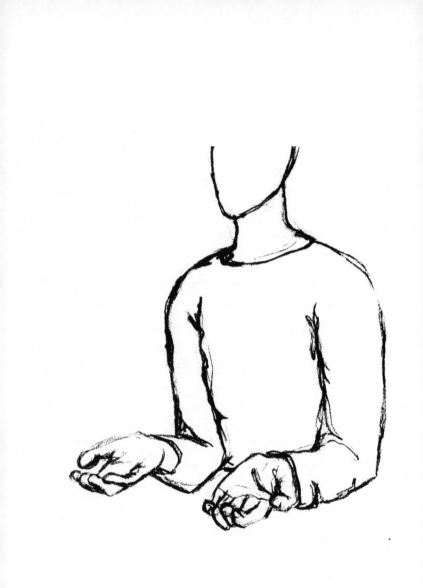

A PRAYER
FOR HEALING

Palms Up

The power of healing is the power of God. When we receive or administer healing, we participate in the work of God. When we plead for healing, we plead with God. This healing can come in an instant or following a last-chance gasp after years of suffering.[1] When we pursue the healing of God for ourselves and for others, we seek both a healing for a season and ultimate healing. When healing comes, we know God is active.[2] So we pray and live as those seeking the healing of God for all creation. We do not suppose to initiate it, but to join in it and draw strength from it.

The power and love of God
Keep us from falling,
Wash us clean,
And place us in the kingdom as pure beings.

PRAYER POSTURE

Stand. Bend your arms in front of you. Make sure your palms are facing up. Point your fingers out straight and spread them apart if you like. Hold your palms as open as you can. Let your open palms be a symbol of your consent to God for healing, and let your fingers point out to the direction of where you want that healing shared.

PRAYER JOURNAL

_____
_____
_____
_____
_____
_____
_____

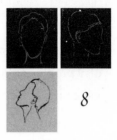

8

A PRAYER FOR COURAGE

Reaching

People of faith are regularly called to have courage. Nearly every time a person in the Bible interacts with God or an angel, that person is urged to have courage. Moses called the nation of Israel to have courage during the Exodus from Egypt. The angels tried to impart courage to wary shepherds at the announcement of the Messiah's birth. Jesus implored his disciples to have courage when he appeared to them after the Resurrection. We could easily conclude that when God is most active, we need the most courage.

Courage is different from confidence. Courage is putting confidence into action; courage breeds action. We pray for courage not to gain confidence but to have the willingness to engage in faith *beyond* our confidence—with a proper confidence. So we pray and live as those with good courage, even faithful courage.

> I want to hear you say I will be more.
> I want the peace that you left us
>> Enveloped in bravery,
>> Dancing with stubborn hope,
>> Whispering promises of strength.
> I want it all—
> Delivered to my home,
> Dropped in my hands.
>
> Until you arrive,
> Until I am invited through the final door,
> I need your help and courage to make it there.

Prayer Posture

Stand with your arms pointed straight down and held next to your body. Hold your palms open and turn them away from you. After a while, bend your elbows and hold your open hands out in front of you at chest level. Next, straighten your arms and hold your hands in front of you at arm's length. Last, lift your arms above your head and reach for what God could drop to you. Reverse the motions as you finish praying. Think about the courage that God gives you, courage that lets you move beyond faith into total and active trust.

Prayer Journal

_____

_____

_____

_____

_____

_____

_____

_____

_____

_____

_____

_____

_____

_____

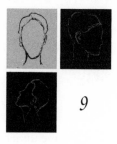

9

A Prayer for Guidance

Sitting with Legs Crossed

T he stories of the faithful are filled with their pleas for guidance. There are those who were guided by a sent star, an appropriate word, or the inner-present Spirit of God. Guidance is a universal and never-ending need. To seek guidance from God is really to seek God, for we are not asking for input from a removed Observer of our lives but from a present and intimately engaged Companion. We find guidance not only amid the broad and generic needs of all humanity but also in the specifics of our own lives. We approach God with assurance and confidence that God is far more interested in guiding us than we are in being guided. We seek and receive guidance from an actively engaged and fully participating Partner in life—One who understands and participates in our experience.[1]

> Speak to me a song of guidance.
> Give me understanding, I pray.

PRAYER POSTURE

Sit on the floor with your legs crossed and pulled close to you. Rest your heels against the inside of your thighs. Place your hands on your knees or on the floor next to your legs, palms facing up. Feel free to engage your head and neck in this prayer posture either by bowing your head and stretching your neck as you lean your head forward or by raising your face to heaven with your eyes open or closed. Meditate on God's wisdom. Remember and seek the many ways that God extends vision, direction, and a clear, open path when guidance is needed.

PRAYER JOURNAL

_____

_____

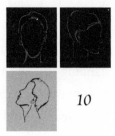

10

A PRAYER

OF RECONCILIATION

Standing Still

I t is God's hope and desire that all creation be reconciled—that is, brought into whole relationship and made compatible with God's intentions for the world. This hope includes people being reconciled with God, people reconciling with one another, and people reconciling with creation.[1] This kind of reconciliation takes hard work and, at times, even requires death and rebirth. Pain often accompanies this bringing together in ways that can seem overwhelming. But the intention of love, faith, and hope is not to overwhelm but to complete, to bring together. At times reconciliation means our moving toward someone or something; at other times reconciliation means standing still and receiving. So we pray and live as those who move when called to move and as those who remain still when we need to remain still—doing it all as participants in the reconciling work of God.

Jesus was not resurrected to what he was,
But was re-created into something new, the risen,
      glorified Christ.
Is there a reconciliation that needs to be completed
Before I am made like my Lord?

I will seek reconciliation; I will go where I need
      to go to find it;
I ask that it be exposed to me.
May the Lord be pleased with my desire
      for wholeness—
In relationship, in grace, in the way of Jesus.
God grant me the wisdom
To know how to best reconcile with each person,
Whether the time is right,
And how to speak the truth in love.
Peace is ahead of my steps; it will be waiting for me.

PRAYER POSTURE

Start in a sitting position. Then use your arms to push your body up so you are standing. Inhale deeply through your mouth. Let your shoulders fall, release any stress in the top of your legs, and let your hips fall forward. Feel pressure on the bottom of your feet—and in that space alone. Let your head fall forward. Relax your face. Relax your hands. Keep breathing deeply. Allow the deep breaths to prepare you and arm you for the work of reconciliation.

PRAYER JOURNAL

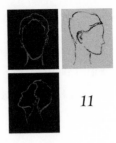

11

A Prayer of Thankfulness

Touching Your Head, Eyes, Hands, Feet

To be thankful is a requisite of life with God. It is essential because when we live without an attitude of thankfulness, life becomes distorted. To be thankful involves more than saying thank you. To be thankful is the full-life recognition that life itself—and so much in it—is a gift. Thankfulness is often the appropriate response to what life brings. From the essence of life in our bodies… to love extended to us from others…to God's grace allowing us to live another day—these are not gifts we can give to ourselves.[1] These things come only from God, and being thankful is the recognition of this reality.

To be thankful is to feel a deep sense of gratefulness that penetrates all of life. It is the recognition of the power of God, the power of people, and the power of love. To be thankful often requires being honest about the nature of life and faith. So we pray and live as grateful people in the midst of a grateful people—or hoping this will be so.

> Lord, in this prayer, I thank you for my body.
> May I use all the abilities in my head to praise you,
> May I see the lives through which you are active in
>   this world,
> May my hands further your story of creation,
> May I walk in the ways you have established.
> For this body, I pray.

PRAYER POSTURE

Stand. Begin this posture from either your head or your feet. Touch your head, eyes, hands, and feet (or do so in reverse order). When touching your head, eyes, hands, or feet, curl your whole hand around that part of your body. Let the warmth or coolness merge from your hands to the body part; hold the touch as long as necessary to feel the interaction between skin touching skin, muscles acting against muscles, cells interacting to make up your body. If you traveled up your body as you prayed, now travel from the top down—or vice versa. Thank God for the gift of life and for the opportunities to participate in the continuing story of God.

PRAYER JOURNAL

_____

_____

_____

_____

_____

_____

_____

_____

_____

_____

_____

_____

_____

_____

_____

_____

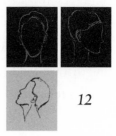

12

A PRAYER FOR AN END

TO LONELINESS

Body Hug

Few experiences are as intense as loneliness, for we were not created to be lonely. To be lonely is to desire companionship but not have it. The good news is that God is not distant or aloof. God is Immanuel, God with us. A peace that exceeds our comprehension comes when we know that we are not alone, that we are surrounded and pursued by God.[1] Not only are we not alone, but we are part of something grand, beautiful, and mystical. The companionship and friendship offered by God allow us to be alone in God's presence without being lonely. We live and pray that we will know the constant presence of God and that we will become to others the physical reminder of God's presence.

> As long as forever is on Earth
> I've been waiting
> For a word, for an answer,
> For arms that don't belong to me
> To promise more than continuing breath.
> My faith is my feet,
> The only way I can keep standing.
> My Rock and my Comforter,
> I pray for assurance that I do not have
>   to do this life alone.

PRAYER POSTURE

Sit down and wrap your arms around yourself, in whatever position is comfortable, and hold yourself. Squeeze if you want to, but be sure to simply feel your arms create warmth and an enclosed, huglike feeling. Contemplate God's constant presence and peace. Feel God's embrace.

Prayer Journal

_____
_____
_____
_____
_____
_____
_____
_____
_____
_____
_____
_____
_____
_____
_____
_____
_____
_____
_____
_____
_____
_____
_____

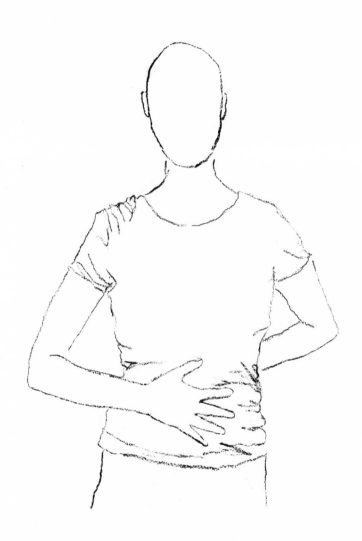

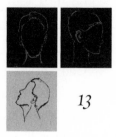

13

A Prayer of Refreshment

Hands on Stomach and Back

Being replenished is an essential part of life. We are created beings in need of rest, food, encouragement, and refreshment. Without refreshment, a life will shrivel and die. This is true of our body and our spirit.

Refreshment brings revival—new beginnings. It can nurture a body, a mind, and a spirit. When we are refreshed, we start anew. So we pray and live as people who seek the refreshment of God in our lives and in the world. We long for God's revitalizing life to be apparent everywhere. We seek goodness from hurt, beauty from ashes, and life from death. Knowing that God will refresh the weary and satisfy the faint sends us into the world with the word of life.[1]

63

God refreshes.
God renews.
God finds beauty in the cast off.
God knows his creation can start anew.
In the ordinary, God is present
And remaking the plain
Into the redeemed.

Prayer Posture

While standing, bend your right arm at a ninety-degree angle and rest your palm flat against your stomach. Bend your left arm at a ninety-degree angle and lay your left palm flat against your back, directly behind and in line with your right hand that is resting against your stomach. Feel the space between your hands…and feel yourself breathe. Take several deep breaths. Switch hands when your arms tire. Allow your hands on your body to serve as a symbol of God's kind, renewing, and thorough touch. Let even the short time when your hands are not on your body be a time of revival and refreshment as your body moves with breath.

PRAYER JOURNAL

_____

_____

_____

_____

_____

_____

_____

_____

_____

_____

_____

_____

_____

_____

_____

_____

_____

_____

_____

_____

_____

_____

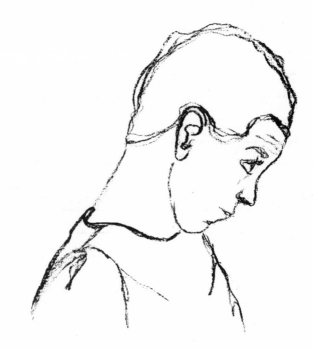

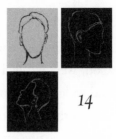

14

A Prayer for

Vulnerability

Bowing Head with Shoulders Back

L iving an open life can be scary. To be dependent upon another person, or even upon God, is not easy, but it is an essential part of a faithful life. When we live well with God and others, we recognize that we *are* needy. To be vulnerable is more than to be held accountable, for in being vulnerable we recognize that we need others to participate in our lives—that we are not designed to handle life on our own. To be vulnerable is to be kept by another and to be one another's keepers.

The life of faith is not intended to be lived in isolation or even in the near vicinity of other people. It is meant to be lived in deep connection with people. As the people of God, we are called to look out for the interests of others and to let others look out for us.[1] So we pray and live to allow others into our lives, and with a readiness to be a redemptive presence in the lives of others.

> I will not let my heart be hardened.
> It is not by my strength that I will prevail.
> The world is not my teacher.
> Whatever I have learned from God, I will put
>   into practice.
> God is mindful of the humble state of his servant.
> The favor of the Lord is upon me.

PRAYER POSTURE

While sitting or standing, extend your neck forward and bow your head. Feel the back of your neck stretch as you face the floor. Deliberately draw your shoulders back—don't hunch forward. Let the muscles of your chest strain while you hold your upper body back and tilt your head forward. Let your extended neck be a symbolic posture of vulnerability and complete submission.

PRAYER JOURNAL

_____

_____

_____

_____

_____

_____

_____

_____

_____

_____

_____

_____

_____

_____

_____

_____

_____

_____

_____

_____

_____

_____

_____

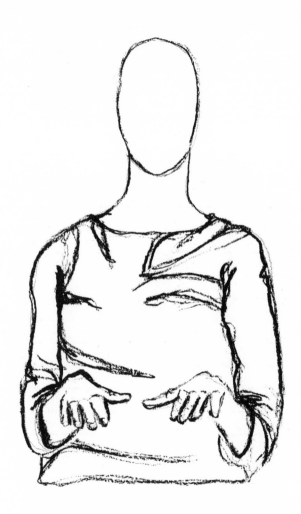

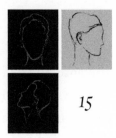

15

A Prayer

for Change

Palms Down

No one day is perfectly like another. Life changes from minute to minute, day to day, year to year. Whether we recognize the changes that take place in our bodies, in our emotions, or in our desires, we know that change is always happening. Change happens within relationships and within each one of us. But this change is not unruly or unguided. God is the God of change.

God brings new life and new hope, and God wants us to live in the rhythm of that new life and to change along with it. We find ourselves playing a part in the midst of God's hopes and intentions for the world. We can call this being born anew, being a new creation.[1] The wonderful assurance is that God will be ever faithful to the promise to always bring about the new. We are not stuck: life is change and change is life, and God engages in all of it. So we pray and live accepting change, seeking change, and being ever changed and engaged by a God who cares for us and who cares about our changes.

> Go in the name of the Lord.
> Believe in the rock churning out water.
> Believe in water changing to wine.
> Believe that you are not alone in your doubts.
> Believe in God's love as stronger than any
>   disbelief.

> Go in the name of the Lord,
> No matter how small the road,
> No matter how undramatic the miracle.
> Go and make believers.
> Go and be healed.
> Go and love your neighbors.
> Go in the name of the Lord.

PRAYER POSTURE

Stand. Lift your straight arms over your head or extend them out in front of you at chest level. Make sure your palms are facing down and your fingers are pointing out straight. Spread your fingers apart. Hold your palms as open as you can for a matter of minutes. Feel life pouring between your fingers, with change coming even when it is unexpected. Meditate on the God who brings change, who welcomes change, who commands change, and who reigns over change.

PRAYER JOURNAL

_____
_____
_____
_____
_____
_____
_____
_____

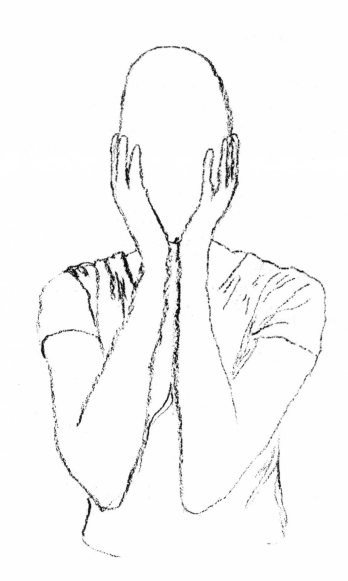

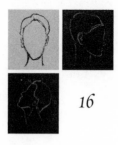

16

A PRAYER FOR BEAUTY

Touching Your Face

There is no end to the beauty of God, to the beauty of the creation of God, or even to the beauty of God within us.[1] As followers of God, we want eyes to see the beauty of God, to reflect the beauty of God, and to live in that beauty. This comes easily when we are surrounded by goodness and love, by God's wondrous creation. At other times we need faith to see how beauty can come from destruction. But the follower of God is ever-reminded of and empowered by the way God brings beauty from the most stained situations. We pray to see the beauty of God and the beauty God can bring to life. We live as the beneficiaries and the beacons of that beauty.

The beauty of the world is fleeting,
But the beauty of God that comes to the world
rests within us.

PRAYER POSTURE

Rest your open hands on your cheeks. Let them remain until both your face and your palms are warmed. Move your hands across, up, and down your face so that you feel all your facial features with your fingers as well as your palms. Remember that God creates all things beautiful. As warmth passes from skin to skin, reflect on the beauty that God gives—which is passing to you and through you.

PRAYER JOURNAL

_____

_____

_____

_____

_____

_____

_____

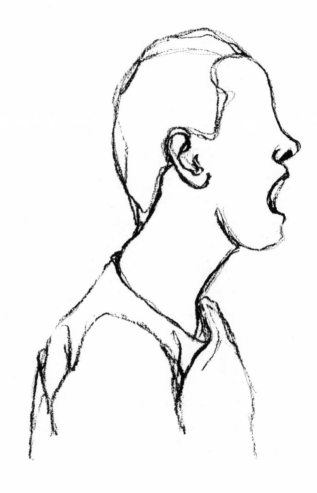

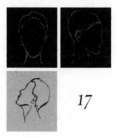

17

A PRAYER FOR MERCY

Mouth Open

The depth and wideness of God's mercy does not originate in us. This mercy extends beyond our inadequacies, failures, and sins—and is not limited by them. This mercy and kindness lead us to repentance and change. Mercy serves as a new beginning, even a remaking. We are not left to our own efforts or compulsions; we are invited into new life. Then we who are shown mercy become the merciful—and blessed are the merciful. May we pray and live in such a way that all would grasp how wide, long, high, and deep is the love of God.[1]

I could use more exhale in my life.
More release. More roads that curve

Where I see you curving them, Lord.
I could use more mornings
When I clearly see your enormity
Before I rise.
Let me see.
Do not withhold your mercy from me.
Let me breathe.

Prayer Posture

Standing tall, tilt your head back slightly and open your mouth as wide as you can. Stretch your lower jaw down and up slightly and notice how foreign it is to have your mouth open that wide. Put your hands on the side of your face, touch your stretched cheeks, and feel the working of your jaw. Consider how mercy can be wide, awkward, and unfamiliar, yet it is always good because it comes from God.

Prayer Journal

_____

_____

_____

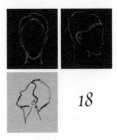

18

A Prayer for Redemption

On Knees and Elbows

Redemption can mean "to repurchase, ransom, release, rescue." It can mean deliverance as well. Redemption is central to our life with God, for God brings release, rescue, and deliverance. God is the Redeemer, the One who finds value where we may not. God liberates and frees us, so that we may fully live into our intention of being active participants in the story of God.[1]

We are pursued and redeemed because we are deeply valued and loved by God. Those of us who understand our value—that we are worthy of redemption—are able to recognize the same value in others. So we pray and live as released people, rescued through the work of the

Redeemer and ever seeking the value in others who are being redeemed.

> For those redeemed, I pray.
> For those in need of redemption, I pray.
> For those unaware
> That you are the Redeemer, I pray.

PRAYER POSTURE

Get down on the floor and support your body with only your elbows and knees. Let your head hang down. Notice the lines created by your bent legs and arms; notice the way your limbs aim in different directions. Feel the pressure between you and the ground, created by the weight of your body. Stretch your neck in the awkwardness of letting your head hang. Meditate on your need to be rescued, to be delivered, to be redeemed.

PRAYER JOURNAL

_____

_____

_____

_____

_____

_____

_____

_____

_____

_____

_____

_____

_____

_____

_____

_____

_____

_____

_____

_____

_____

_____

_____

_____

_____

_____

_____

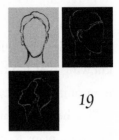

19

A Prayer of Willingness

Rag-Doll Bend

Faith may well be understood as the willingness to follow. Christian faith is following God in the way of Jesus and involves far more than simply believing the right things; Christianity is a lived faith.[1] The faithful people in the Bible realized this, and that story is told from Abraham's being willing to leave his homeland for a new land, to Mary's declaring that she was the servant of the Lord, to Jesus' saying "Your will be done" during the week of his death.

Our willingness to follow the leading of God ranks as one of the most difficult and important aspects of praying and living with God. But this willingness is not drudgery; we are not leaving behind something better in order to follow God. Faithful willingness to follow comes from knowing that God's plans, dreams, and desires are better than ours, that they are the best way to go. To pray for a willing heart is to pray a promise: "I know the plans I have for you...plans to give you hope and a future."[2]

> In the Extraordinary that is you,
> I breathe.
> I breathe and I bend.
> I breathe and I bend and I dream
> Of seeing your will clearly,
> Of following you easily,
> Of hearing
> Finales to the world's worries
> And beginnings to untold stories.
> Until those whispers are rumbled,
> When they resound as Truth echoed by all cells,
> I submit to you.

Prayer Posture

Stand, then lean over at the waist as far as you can without moving your feet. Let your shoulders, arms, neck, and head all fall forward and hang very loosely. Let your body re-arrange itself according to its weight. Permit your body's looseness to echo your submission to God. Consider how your flexibility symbolizes the letting go that is the sub-mission, the release of all things, necessary for emptying your hands and receiving what God wants for you. As you stand before God, be willing.

Prayer Journal

_____

_____

_____

_____

_____

_____

_____

_____

_____

_____

_____

_____

_____

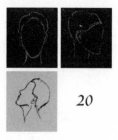

20

A Prayer for the Poor

Kneeling

God's concern has always been for those who are poor—poor in spirit, poor in hope, poor in food, poor in connection, and poor in love. God is not only concerned but present with the poor, for blessed are the poor.[1] When we join the activity of God, we join with those who go without. Our prayer is not only *for* the poor, but we pray *as* the poor—for we are all lacking in what we need. In this recognition we find the life of God.

We live in community to share our needs—as well as our resources—with others. We live and pray not only to fill needs but to join with the poor, our brothers and sisters, in being cared for and in providing for others.

Life with God is never satisfied only with reaching out

in pity to offer help or in desperation to ask for help. We join with the needy, the poor, because we are part of them.

> I ask that you bless those who are needy
> With roofs when it rains,
> With food and drink when wants arise,
> With care when it cannot be bought.
> I ask for our friends who have less than the world's
>   standards
> To know that they are loved,
> To rest in knowing that they are not alone
>   in figuring out life,
> To be surrounded by your tireless, guarding love.

PRAYER POSTURE

Kneel on the floor facing a chair or low table. Rest your elbows on the chair or table and hold your face in your hands. (If you don't have anything in front of you, rest your elbows on your thighs and cradle your face in your hands.) Pray not for people who are different from you but pray as one community—for needs, for the endless delivery of God's nourishments and provisions.

Prayer Journal

_____
_____
_____
_____
_____
_____
_____
_____
_____
_____
_____
_____
_____
_____
_____
_____
_____
_____
_____
_____
_____
_____
_____
_____

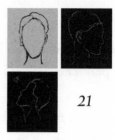

21

A Prayer

for God's Activity

in the Lives of Others

Rubbing Palms Together Vigorously

There is no limit to God's creative activity. From the start of the universe with God's creation of space and matter out of a formless void…to the breath of life in our lungs…to the power of God that resurrects the dead, there is no end to the life and energy of God. As those who seek the life of God in our world, we pray and live in a way that welcomes, invites, and longs for the intentions of God to be fulfilled today, as it was in the beginning. God invites us to join with God our hopes, prayers, and bodies. May we be people who live by the energy of God, and may our prayer extend to those who need God's power in their lives.

Let my words be a blessing,
Let the energy of God be the energy within me,
Let God's presence in my life define my life.

PRAYER POSTURE

While you're sitting or standing, extend your fingers and rub your palms together furiously for ten seconds or more. Then, holding your hands open with your fingers straight, separate your palms less than an inch apart and feel the warmth between your palms. Think about God's creative activity in your life. Think as well about God's energy at work in you and passing through you to others. Think of those people who need God to act on their behalf.

PRAYER JOURNAL

_____

_____

_____

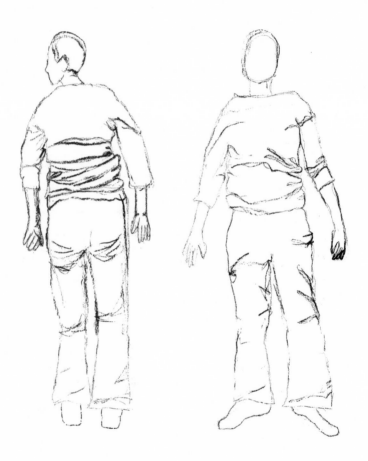

22

A Prayer for Hope

in the Journey

Lying Faceup, Facedown

God leads us on a journey, but often we don't understand where we are headed until we arrive. There are no maps for the journey of life. Instead there is a call, a presence, a wholeness, and a blessing to be given to us and through us as we travel.

We hope God will clearly show us this road, but it may take a lifetime of promises made and broken, lives lived and lost, faith strengthened and remade before we finally recognize the place God is leading us to. As we travel, we find hope not only in the destination but also in the journey. We do not travel alone. Like the nation of

Israel, we live and pray, looking for the leading of God as we struggle forward through the wilderness.[1]

Leaving your place of comfort and familiarity and going to a place where God leads is rarely simple or easy. But for all of history, this has been the situation of those who live in the rhythm of God. So we pray and live today as those on the journey of God.

With you and to you, Jesus,
I hope and I follow.

Prayer Posture

Begin by lying on your stomach. Put your arms at your sides. Make sure your arms, the top of your feet, and your forehead are against the floor. Stay in the posture for at least thirty seconds. (A recommended way to count a half minute is to use this prayer: *With you and to you, Jesus,* ONE *I hope and I follow,* TWO.) After praying to thirty, turn over on your back. Bend your knees if that is a more comfortable position for you. While praying for another thirty seconds, note how much easier it is to breathe and how much cooler the air tastes when you are facing up. Our hope is above, with our Guide in the journey.

Prayer Journal

_____

_____

_____

_____

_____

_____

_____

_____

_____

_____

_____

_____

_____

_____

_____

_____

_____

_____

23

A PRAYER

OF PRESERVATION

Hands Resting atop Your Head

The good work that God has begun, God will complete.[1] We can see this truth in our lives and in nature. We can and should live with the confidence that God is going to stay involved and engaged in our lives. So we extend to the rest of the world this hope: that good will be saved and increased and that God's dreams will be done on earth as they are in heaven. When we find ourselves wondering whether all goodness will fall away or if it will be short-lived, may we be people of prayerful confidence that God will bless us and keep us, that God will make God's face shine upon us and give us peace.[2]

We rest, our Keeper of Promises,
In the words you laid on us generations ago.
We believe that you will bless us,
We believe that you will keep us,
We believe that as a people who follow your Way,
We will continue your blessings to others.

PRAYER POSTURE

While standing, interlace your fingers and rest your open hands (palms down) on the top of your head. Feel the pressure of your arms on your body. As you stand in prayer, feel God's hands on and over you, hands full of goodness, protection, and preservation.

PRAYER JOURNAL

_____

_____

_____

_____

_____

_____

_____
_____
_____
_____
_____
_____
_____
_____
_____
_____
_____
_____
_____
_____
_____
_____
_____
_____
_____
_____
_____
_____
_____
_____
_____
_____

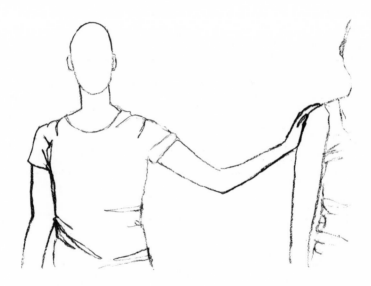

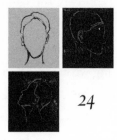

24

A Prayer

for Connectedness,

Community, Friendship

Hands Extended to Another

The wonder of God's creation is found within the connections of life. Because all creation is the work of God, all creation is connected. There is no place we can go that is not in the purview of God.

The connections within God's creation add to the wonder of faith. Seeing these connections and living in them is part of a faith being built, as happened when the followers of Jesus misunderstood the connections involved in the life of the man who was born blind. They wondered aloud whose sin had caused the man's disability, connecting wrongdoing with his blindness. Jesus said this was not the case. There was a greater story going on. The glory of God was going to be revealed in the blind man's life.[1] Connections also become visible in the reconciling work of Jesus that connects the past with the future.[2]

When we seek to pray and live as people who are connected to one another, to creation, and simultaneously to our past and future, we become people of growing faith.

> May the road God has laid
> Rise up to meet you.
> May God keep you and bless you,
> Shine his light upon you,
> And give you peace.

PRAYER POSTURE

Lay hands on another person and let them represent God's hands resting on us and connecting us to one another. Or, as a symbol of the hands of God resting on you, gently rest your hand on your own shoulder, head, or leg while you pray.

Prayer Journal

_____

_____

_____

_____

_____

_____

_____

_____

_____

_____

_____

_____

_____

_____

_____

_____

_____

_____

_____

_____

_____

_____

_____

_____

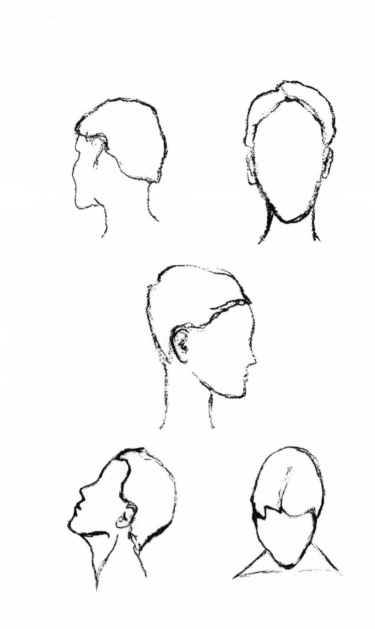

25

A Prayer for Eyes

to See God's Work

Looking Back, Forward, to the Side, Up, Down

Throughout history people of faith have sought to see and understand in the same way that God sees and understands. Being created in the image of God, we are endowed with the desire to live in harmony with God. So we seek to have eyes to see and ears to hear what God is about in the world.[1]

We live and pray as people who want to see the work of God in the world, to have the mind of Christ, and to be ever aware of all that God is about, so that we may offer ourselves as living participants in the life of God.

Give us your eyes
As we approach the season of your coming.
Give us your eyes
As we learn to love in the way of your love.
Give us your eyes
In our homes, our churches, and outward
      in the world.
Give us your eyes.
Let us see your presence in all of us.

Prayer Posture

To begin, stand and face forward. While you pray, turn your head in all directions: as far behind you as possible, then to both sides, then up, and then down. Finish your prayer by again facing forward. With each turn of your head, invite God to let you see with God's loving eyes— other people, nature, or whatever else surrounds you.

Prayer Journal

_____

_____

_____

_____

_____

_____

_____

_____

_____

_____

_____

_____

_____

_____

_____

_____

_____

_____

_____

_____

_____

_____

_____

_____

_____

_____

_____

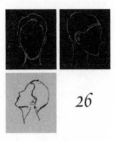

26

A PRAYER OF FORGIVENESS

Deliberate Breathing

Few descriptions of God have the beauty and nuance of the word *breath*. Thinking of God as the Breath of Life helps us understand that God is within us.[1] The word *breath* takes us to the story of God's creating humankind with a breath and to Jesus' breathing the Holy Spirit upon the disciples.

In the same way that breath fills our body and gives us life, so forgiveness fills our soul and gives us life. As with breathing, forgiveness exhales the old, the sin, and then inhales clean, nurturing air—acceptance, love, and compassion. We need forgiveness just as we need air, and forgiveness is just as available. God breathed life into humankind and called it very good, and God breathes forgiveness into us for the same purpose—life and goodness.

There is no limit to forgiveness for us or from us. Jesus taught his followers to forgive not the customary number of times but a never-ending number of times.[2] We can become those who are refreshed by forgiveness and those who extend it to others—we breathe it in, and we breathe it out.

> Holy Spirit, lead us in reflecting you:
> Through the air we breathe and through our
>   bodies,
> May we move in the way you would like us
>   to move.
> May we breathe in the forgiveness of Jesus,
> His gentle release of sins.
> May we give others the same breath of release.

PRAYER POSTURE

Stand with your feet shoulder-width apart and feel your bones sink into the ground. Breathe in slowly through your nose, feeling your diaphragm compress as you inhale.

Exhale slowly through your mouth or your nose, feeling your stomach flatten as the air flows out of you. Continue breathing, meditating on the life-giving grace of God's forgiveness as you breathe in, and on the grace of God in you to forgive others as you breathe out.

PRAYER JOURNAL

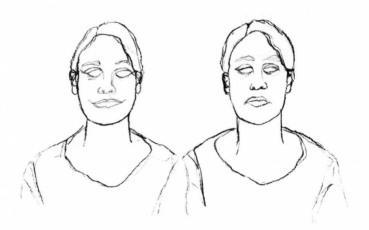

27

A PRAYER TO BECOME

A BLESSING

Smiling and Relaxing Your Face

God's call to Abraham, the patriarch of faith, is the call extended to all humankind: be a blessing to all the world. God told Abraham, "All peoples on earth will be blessed through you."[1] When we accept the call of God to be a blessing, we are blessed to be distributors of the goodness of God. We are loved by God, and in turn we love; we are forgiven, and in turn we forgive; we are made whole, and in turn we make others whole. When we count our blessings it is the beginning of prayer, not the end. We ask God to bless others not simply for their satisfaction and fulfillment but so they can join in blessing others.

May we live so that all peoples on earth will be blessed through us.[2]

> I raise my lips as an offering.
> Silently, I give my God
> The front— the top— the first impression
> of who I am.
> My best; the way he chose to present me.
> I ask you, Lord, to use me in giving, in healing,
> in blessing.

PRAYER POSTURE

Whether standing or sitting, take a deep breath through your nose and relax your shoulders. Relax your jaw, your cheekbones, and the tension in your forehead and around your eyes. Breathe in through your nose and out through your mouth. Close your eyes. Raise the corners of your mouth and feel your cheeks rise. Lower the corners of your mouth, then part your lips and grin, showing all your teeth. Hold that pose for five seconds. Finally, relax your face again and open your eyes while your face is still loose. Hold on to the feeling of relaxation in your face. Let that ease guide you in blessing all who share the world with you.

PRAYER JOURNAL

_____

_____

_____

_____

_____

_____

_____

_____

_____

_____

_____

_____

_____

_____

_____

_____

_____

_____

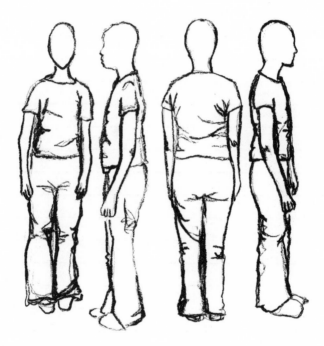

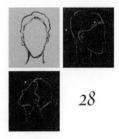

A Prayer to Become

Useful in God's Plan

Facing the Four Directions

From the earliest days of Christianity, followers under-stood that pure and lasting religion in the sight of God means that we must care for orphans and widows in their troubles and refuse to let the world corrupt us.[1] This kind of faith contributes not only to our own fulfillment but also benefits those in need.

When we ask God to use us in the kingdom of God, we are invited to know and be the good news of God. We pray and live in the hope that we will be part of what God is doing and that our lives will be a benefit and blessing to the entire world.

I rejoice in your stories of redemption
To the north, to the south, to the east, and
      to the west.
I live in your victory over sin
In the north, the south, the east, and the west.
I extend your invitations to Life
In the north, the south, the east, and the west.
I rest in hallelujah
In the north, the south, the east, and the west.
I leave behind me your promise of peace
In the north, the south, the east, and the west.
I rejoice in amen
In your north, your south, your east, and your
      west.

PRAYER POSTURE

Stand outside if possible. Begin your prayer by turning your body toward the north. Look at the whole of the direction—scanning your eyes on the horizon from side to side, up and down. Then turn your body to the three other directions and do the same deliberate looking, at every element in front of you. As you observe what is before you, open yourself to the ways in which God desires to use you.

PRAYER JOURNAL

_____

_____

_____

_____

_____

_____

_____

_____

_____

_____

_____

_____

_____

_____

_____

_____

_____

_____

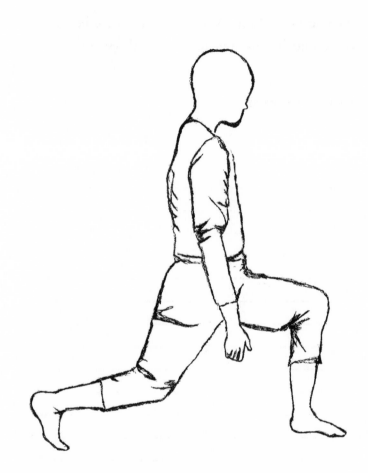

29

A Prayer for the

Rhythm of God

Stepping Forward

There is a rhythm to life. We find it in the ocean tides, in the rising and setting of the sun, in the beating of our hearts. And there is a rhythm of God—a rhythm that encompasses life, both the life we can readily see and the unseen life of the spirit. The rhythm of God beckons us, guides us, and dwells in us. When we discover the rhythm of God, we find the heart of God, the dreams of God, the will of God. As those who are created in the image of God, we are endowed with this rhythm. We can find it, step into it, and live in it. This is the kingdom of God—to live in sync with the rhythm of God.[1] We pray and live to seek not only the specifics of God's will but also the song, the rhythm of God: we seek to walk in it.

> The Lord our God
> Sets our feet in spacious places,
> Delivers us from evil,
> Has given us freedom with the opening of his hand.
> Let us lean into the future before us.
> Let us follow the Way.

PRAYER POSTURE

Begin by standing with your feet together and your arms hanging at your sides. With either your left or right foot, lunge forward far enough to feel the stretch in your thigh. If you can, lower the thigh of the leg in front to create a ninety-degree angle in the bend of your knee. Switch legs after a while if you need to. Feel the rhythm of God in your muscles as they strain, in your legs as you switch position, in your breathing, and in the breathing and sounds of those around you. As you let the rhythm created in the room around you expand in your mind, consider how the rhythm of God is all around us.

PRAYER JOURNAL

_____
_____
_____
_____
_____
_____
_____
_____
_____
_____
_____
_____
_____
_____
_____
_____
_____
_____
_____
_____
_____
_____
_____

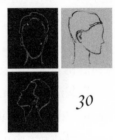

30

A PRAYER FOR GLOBAL

TRANSFORMATION

Pulling Clasped Hands

The complexities of the world are endless; the complexities of our own lives are ceaseless. We are called to live as a people who not only speak of what is, but of what is to come—the full transformation of all of life. We profess our hopes, desires, and beliefs not as people who are certain of the means of this transformation but as those who long for it.

We profess that God wants goodness for the world and that God works for the salvation of the earth and all who are in it.[1] We know that creation is not complete but that it is in the midst of re-creation. So we pray for our world to grow into the fullness that God desires for it. May God's kingdom come; may God's will be done. We live in the world; we join in its re-creation. We pray and live with the confidence that God will continue the good work that has been started.

> Our Lord is the Lord of all.
> In goodness and in evil, the Lord reigns.
> In peace and in war, the Lord reigns.
> In health and in illness, the Lord reigns.
> In the simple and in the inexplicable, our Lord
>   is the Lord who reigns.

Prayer Posture

While standing, hook your fingers together, one hand underneath the other, with your hands clasped at chest height. Cradle your fingers and pull. You should feel tension in your chest, shoulders, and upper arms. Contemplate the tension that creation experiences as it awaits God's work of re-creation.

PRAYER JOURNAL

_____

_____

_____

_____

_____

_____

_____

_____

_____

_____

_____

_____

_____

_____

_____

_____

_____

_____

_____

_____

Appendix A

BIBLE REFERENCES

The following Bible references are pertinent to the prayers in this book. You are invited to use these verses to add context and deeper meaning in conjunction with the prayer postures.

One
Colossians 3:12-13

Two
Matthew 17:20; Psalm 73:26; Philippians 4:13

Three
Psalm 113

Four

Matthew 6:9-14; John 14:27

Five

The Nicene Creed

We believe in one God,
the Father, the Almighty,
maker of heaven and earth,
of all that is, seen and unseen.

We believe in one Lord, Jesus Christ,
the only Son of God,
eternally begotten of the Father,
God from God, Light from Light,
true God from true God,
begotten, not made,
of one Being with the Father.
Through him all things were made.
For us and for our salvation
he came down from heaven:

by the power of the Holy Spirit
he became incarnate from the Virgin Mary,
and was made man.
For our sake he was crucified under Pontius
Pilate;
he suffered death and was buried.
On the third day he rose again
in accordance with the Scriptures;
he ascended into heaven
and is seated at the right hand of the Father.
He will come again in glory to judge the living
and the dead,
and his kingdom will have no end.
We believe in the Holy Spirit, the Lord, the giver
of life,
who proceeds from the Father and the Son.
With the Father and the Son he is worshiped
and glorified.
He has spoken through the Prophets.
We believe in one holy catholic and apostolic
Church.
We acknowledge one baptism for the forgiveness
of sins.

We look for the resurrection of the dead,
and the life of the world to come. Amen.

"The Nicene Creed," *The Book of Common Prayer* (New York: The Church Hymnal Corporation, 1979), 358-59.

Six
Psalm 28:6-7

Seven
Jude 24-25

Eight
John 14:1; Philippians 1:19-21; Joshua 1:6-7

Nine
Luke 24:36-49

Ten
2 Corinthians 5:17-21

Eleven
John 1:1,4; Acts 2:26; Romans 6:13

Twelve
Psalm 62

Thirteen
Isaiah 61:1-3

Fourteen
Daniel 5:18-23; Jeremiah 20:7-13; Colossians 3:16;
Philippians 2:3-8; Luke 1:46-55

Fifteen
Exodus 17:1-5; John 2:1-11; Matthew 28:18-20; Luke
8:47-49; Leviticus 19; Psalm 118:25-26

Sixteen
Genesis 1:31; Isaiah 61:1-3

Seventeen
Isaiah 63:7-9

Eighteen
Isaiah 63:15-17

Nineteen
Luke 1:38; 22:41-44

Twenty
Leviticus 25:35; Deuteronomy 15:11; Psalm 35:9-11;
Luke 4:17-19

Twenty-One
Genesis 1:1-2,31; 2:7

Twenty-Two
Luke 9:56-58; Romans 15:4-6

Twenty-Three
Numbers 6:24-26

Twenty-Four
Numbers 6:22-27; traditional Irish blessing:

> May the road rise to meet you.
> May the wind be always at your back.
> May the sun shine warm upon your face

And rains fall soft upon your fields.

And until we meet again,

May God hold you in the hollow of his hand.

Twenty-Five

Philippians 2:13; 4:19-20

Twenty-Six

Ephesians 3:16-19; Titus 3:4-8

Twenty-Seven

Ephesians 5:1-3; Genesis 12:2-3

Twenty-Eight

Genesis 13:14-18

Twenty-Nine

Matthew 6:9-14; Psalm 31; Deuteronomy 5:15; Malachi 3:1; John 14:5-7

Thirty

Psalm 146:10; Romans 8:18-22; Isaiah 58

Appendix B

Prayer Topics

The poetic prayers in this book come in three kinds: meditative, requesting, and prophetic. Additionally, each prayer focuses on a particular need or topic. Following are the thirty prayers grouped according to the type of prayer, and with the topic of each prayer indicated. The chapter number is provided after each prayer topic.

Meditative Prayers

Beauty (16)

Becoming Useful in God's Plan (28)

Connectedness, Community, Friendship (24)

Enjoyment (3)

God's Activity in the Lives of Others (21)

Guidance (9)

Hopefulness (5)

Hope in the Journey (22)

Kindness (1)

Praise (6)

Re-Creation (4)

Vulnerability (14)

Willingness (19)

Prophetic Prayers

Change (15)

Global Transformation (30)

Preservation (23)

Rhythm of God (29)

Strength (2)

Thankfulness (11)

Requesting Prayers

Becoming a Blessing (27)

Courage (8)

End to Loneliness (12)

Eyes to See God's Work (25)

Forgiveness (26)

Healing (7)

THE PRAYER POSTURES

Following are the thirty bodyprayers listed alphabetically by prayer posture. The chapter number is provided after each one.

Notes

Introduction

The epigraph is taken from Luke 10:27, MSG.

1. Colossians 1:19.
2. Doug Pagitt and the Solomon's Porch Community, *Reimagining Spiritual Formation* (Grand Rapids: Zondervan, 2004), 70. (This book will be released in August 2005 with a new title: *Church Re-Imagined.*)
3. Pagitt, *Reimagining,* 71.

One

1. See Galatians 5:22-23.

Three

1. See John 10:10.

Four

1. See Romans 8:22-24.
2. See 2 Corinthians 5:1-2.

Five

    1. See 1 Corinthians 13:13.

Six

    1. See Romans 1–2.

    2. See Genesis 1; Ephesians 3.

Seven

    1. See Luke 8:28-29,38-39,46-48,53-55.

    2. See Matthew 11:4-5.

Nine

    1. See Hebrews 4:15.

Ten

    1. See 2 Corinthians 5:17-21.

Eleven

    1. See Ephesians 2:4-5,8-10.

Twelve

    1. See Philippians 4:5-7.

Thirteen

1. See Jeremiah 31:12-14.

Fourteen

1. See Philippians 2:3-8.

Fifteen

1. See 2 Corinthians 5:17.

Sixteen

1. See 1 Peter 3:3-4.

Seventeen

1. See Ephesians 3:17-19.

Eighteen

1. See 1 Corinthians 1:30-31.

Nineteen

1. See James 2:14-18.
2. Jeremiah 29:11.

Twenty

1. See Matthew 5:3; 10:8,42.

Twenty-Two

1. See Exodus 13:20-22.

Twenty-Three

1. See Philippians 1:6.
2. See Numbers 6:24-26.

Twenty-Four

1. See John 9:1-3.
2. See Hebrews 5:1-6.

Twenty-Five

1. See Mark 4:9; Revelation 2:29.

Twenty-Six

1. See Revelation 11:11; Genesis 2:7.
2. See Matthew 18:21-22.

Twenty-Seven

1. Genesis 12:3.
2. See Mark 12:31.

Twenty-Eight

1. James 1:27, author's paraphrase.

Twenty-Nine

1. See Galatians 5:25.

Thirty

1. See 1 Timothy 2:1-6.